Crime

Judith Anderson

W
FRANKLIN WATTS
LONDON • SYDNEY

First published in 2009 by
Franklin Watts
338 Euston Road
London NW1 3BH

Franklin Watts Australia
Level 17/207 Kent Street
Sydney NSW 2000

Series editor: Julia Bird
Design: Nimbus Design

A CIP catalogue record for this book is available
from the British Library.

ISBN 978 0 7496 8867 7

Dewey classification: 364

Picture credits:
Aberystwyth/Alamy: 38; John Birdsall/PAI: 15, 36; Mike Booth/Alamy: 18;
CBS/Everett/Rex Features: 40; Caroline Contino/BEI/Rex Features: 27;
David Fisher/Rex Features: 32; John Giles/PA Archive/PAI: 33; Garry He/AP/PAI: 19.
Jeremy Horner/Corbis: 34; Hulton-Deutsch/Corbis: 8; Lenny Iguelz/AP/PAI: 10.
Image Source/Rex Features: 11; Nils Jorgensen/Rex Features: 41.
KPA/Zuma/Rex Features: 9; Dominic Lipinski/PAI: 12; Ilene MacDonald/Alamy: 13.
Rick Maiman/Sygma/Corbis: 17; Toby Melville/Corbis: 24; Murray/Rex Features: 22.
Tracey Nearmy/epa/Corbis: 21; PA Archive/PAI: 14; Chris Radburn/PA Archive/ PAI: 26;
Rex Features: 29, 37; Laura Segall/NY Times/Reducx Pictures/Eyevine: 28;
Alex Segre/Alamy: 39; Sipa Press/Rex Features: 25, 31; Ted Soqui/Corbis: 23.
Steve Starr/Corbis: 16; STR/epa/Corbis: 30; Jean-Michel Turpin/Corbis: 20.
Danny Young/Rex Features: 35.

Every attempt has been made to clear copyright.
Should there be any inadvertent omission,
please apply to the publisher for rectification.

Printed in Malaysia

Franklin Watts is a division of Hachette Children's Books,
an Hachette UK company.
www.hachette.co.uk

Contents

Crime:
a public interest

Crime concerns us all. We want to feel safe and finding out about crime helps us to protect ourselves against it. We are curious, too, about things that we hope will never happen to us. Fortunately, most people don't experience crime on a regular basis. So we look to the media to tell us about it.

Case study: The impact of television

The spread of television in the mid-twentieth century brought serious crime into people's living rooms for the first time. This was highlighted by the murders of five children that took place in the north of England in the mid-1960s. Television crews followed the police as they searched the open countryside for bodies in a case the media dubbed 'the Moors murders'. When Ian Brady and Myra Hindley were convicted of the murders, their photographs appeared on news bulletins around the world. Television audiences followed the case and absorbed the horrifying details. Because of the intense media coverage they received, the Moors murders have never been forgotten. They have also been blamed for the increasing fear about children's safety that is still with us today.

This photograph of Moors murderer Myra Hindley has been reproduced so often that it is one of the most famous images of the 1960s.

The media's response

Editors and programme-makers respond to this demand for information. TV news programmes, documentaries, films and newspapers and the radio are full of stories about the bad things that people do. Sometimes the most shocking or extreme crimes are the ones we want to know about most. And the media thrives on giving us what we want.

A false impression?

The crimes that get the most attention in the media are not usually the most common ones. This is because most people are far more interested in a serious crime like murder than in 'everyday' crimes like vandalism or theft. Murder is actually very rare in most neighbourhoods, but the media coverage that it receives can create the impression that it is far more widespread.

• Up for discussion •

An Australian TV programme called *Crime Investigation Australia* reconstructs gruesome murders, while many other TV channels around the world broadcast 'real-life' crimes. Why do you think these programmes choose to focus on murder and violence?

What type of crime concerns you most?

The murder of child beauty queen JonBenet Ramsay in the US in 1996 received intense media coverage. Her attacker has never been caught, though journalists have speculated at length about who killed her.

What's new?

Every year seems to bring a new 'crime wave'. Dramatic headlines help to focus our attention on the latest fear: knife or gun crime; car jacking; drug crime; illegal immigration. We want to know what's new and what's changing, and the media wants to keep us interested.

Crimes such as illegal immigration have been around for a long time, but pictures such as this can create the impression that they are a new threat.

New threats

The media reflects public opinion, but it also informs people about new threats. Where this is done responsibly, it provides a vital public service in the fight against crime. Twenty years ago there was no Internet crime, because there was no Internet. Now people are much more aware of the need to protect themselves against identity theft and online fraud because of the way these issues have been highlighted in the media.

Changing attitudes

Of course, crime has always existed. Yet public attitudes towards different types of behaviour change over time. Our laws about drugs, sex, violence in the home, racial prejudice and homophobia have all undergone huge transformations in the past 100 years. In the nineteenth century, the author Oscar Wilde was imprisoned for practising homosexuality after a trial that was sensationalised by the media. Race discrimination, on the other hand,

Case study: Hoodies

Over the last few years, young people who wear 'hoodies' – hooded tops – have become associated with a perceived rise in antisocial behaviour. This is because a hoodie can obscure the wearer's face, preventing identification by CCTV cameras or members of the public. As a result, hooded tops have been banned from many US schools and even some shopping centres in the UK – whether or not the wearer is behaving suspiciously. The word 'hoodie' has become a form of media shorthand used in news headlines to express a public fear of young people. However, many hoodie-wearers argue that this is an unfair stereotype that ignores the real issues and statistics about crime.

• Up for discussion •

What types of crime do you think are on the increase? Why?

Some argue that headlines such as 'Hoodie thugs' increase our fear of crime, while others say that the media simply reflects public opinion about crime. What do you think?

was not a crime and was not reported. Nowadays, many countries have laws to protect people from different forms of prejudice and the media tends to reflect our changing attitudes.

Are hoodie-wearers more likely to be criminals, or is this a media stereotype?

Fighting crime

The police, government and other anti-crime campaigners frequently use the media to help them fight crime. Sometimes they place adverts in newspapers or on TV, or make appearances on TV or radio to put their message across. Often they set up a press conference to highlight a crime story and attract media attention.

The press conference

The police will call a press conference when they want to put out an appeal for information or witnesses, or because they want to put pressure on offenders and their families to come forward. The media are invited to ask questions, take photographs, reproduce CCTV images and put across the police's version of events. They might also be asked to publicise a telephone hotline or a website set up to deal with a particular case. Most media organisations are very willing to take part. The police get the publicity they want and the media get a news story. Sometimes, however, the police will request a 'news blackout' from the media, particularly if the crime involves hostages or kidnap victims.

British woman Lindsay Hawker was murdered in Japan in 2007. Her family gave press conferences to appeal for help in finding her killer.

Case study: Drink-driving campaigns

Be Safe...
If impaired by alcohol or drugs
DON'T DRIVE
An average of 4 Canadians die daily as a result of impaired driving.
MADD Stop impaired drivers... CALL 911

A MADD billboard in the US alongside white crosses to highlight the number of people killed by drink-drivers.

Every year, the police and other campaigners, such as the US group MADD (Mothers Against Drink Driving), use the media to tackle the crime of drink-driving. Campaigns are given catchy titles such as 'Highways or dieways?' and 'Sober or slammer?' and press conferences are set up in hospitals to highlight the dangers. A social awareness campaign launched in Canada in 2008 used a series of web-based videos known as 'Paul's Story'. The videos told the story of a fictional teenager, Paul, coping with the consequences of killing and injuring his friends after drink-driving. Facebook pages and blogs were used to extend the campaign.

New media

The police are increasingly turning to video-sharing Internet sites such as YouTube to place appeals for information, CCTV footage of suspects and short films about the dangers of drugs or carrying weapons. These sites are seen as important tools by some campaigners, not only because they are more likely to reach a young audience, but also because they can appear quite amateurish or homemade, with more appeal for those who might distrust or ignore an 'official' message.

• Up for discussion •

Some anti-crime campaigns emphasise the consequences for the victims of crime – death, injury, trauma and so on. Other campaigns focus on the consequences for the perpetrators – prison, fines and public disgrace. Which type of campaign do you think is most effective? Why?

Your call counts!

Some TV shows are made with the help of the police. They aim to discover new leads for unsolved crimes by encouraging viewers to phone in with information. Shows like *Crimewatch* and *America's Most Wanted* broadcast interviews with witnesses, re-enactments of crimes and CCTV footage in order to jog people's memories.

A public service

The producers of these shows say that they are performing a public service with a good success rate in terms of convictions. Members of the public may call anonymously, and all new information is examined carefully by the police. The programme-makers do not usually offer a reward. However, the success of the show depends on the size of the audience. The more people watch, the better the level of response. Some people think that the pressure to attract large audiences may distort the way some crimes are presented.

Featured crimes

Which crimes do the programme-makers choose to feature? British show *Crimewatch*'s producers have said that the police must be able to present a new angle or lead for a case to be broadcast. And, of course, crimes are more 'watchable' if the programme contains exciting visual evidence or re-enactments. Tragically, *Crimewatch* presenter Jill Dando was murdered by an unknown assailant in 1999. The show that featured a reconstruction of her murder was one of the most watched in the history of the series.

Crimewatch presenter Jill Dando was murdered in 1999. Her killer has never been caught.

Case study: Crime Stoppers

Crime Stoppers is a not-for-profit community organisation that works with the local police and media to solve crimes.

Crime Stoppers began in Albuquerque, New Mexico in 1976 when a police detective called Greg MacAleese reached a dead-end in a murder investigation. Frustrated by the lack of clues, he turned to the media and persuaded a local television station to produce a re-enactment of the crime. Within 72 hours of the re-enactment being aired, the police received a tip that helped solve the murder.

The Crime Stoppers concept is now widespread in many countries, including the US, UK, Canada and Australia. Members of the public can call a hotline anonymously and leave information. If this leads to an arrest, the informant can claim a cash reward but only if they request one. The informant is then given a code number so that their identity stays secret.

A Crime Stoppers billboard in the US offers anonymity and a cash reward in exchange for information.

• Up for discussion •

Many TV programmes such as *Crimewatch* show detailed reconstructions of crimes. Do you think people watch them for information, or entertainment? Does it matter?

The thrill
of the chase

The success of any media output depends on the size of its audience. But TV programmes, websites or newspapers are competing against each other for a share of that audience. So how can a media outlet gain an advantage over its rivals?

A dangerous pursuit

Many news organisations seek to improve their audience ratings by being the first to break the news, being closest to the action and providing the most dramatic coverage of events as they unfold. Some news networks dispatch helicopters to follow police response vehicles when a crime is committed. They hope to film the action from above. Car chases are particularly popular as they can be followed from the air and generally result in arrests on the ground after some spectacularly dangerous driving. However, several TV crews may end up following the same car and in 2007 four people were killed in Arizona, USA, when two helicopters from rival networks collided in mid-air.

Police, Camera, Action!

A number of TV shows rely on video footage of car chases supplied to them by the police, usually for a fee. Where this occurs, the police usually point out that the fees are spent on road safety improvements and that such programmes help

Helicopters carrying TV crews can transmit live coverage to audiences keen to catch the action.

• Up for discussion •

Do programmes showing high speed police car chases encourage dangerous driving or do they provide a public service? Why are they so popular?

to educate the public by showing the consequences of criminal behaviour when suspects are caught and arrested.

However, some people argue that the presence of cameras in the sky or on the ground simply encourages the police to initiate more chases, making criminals attempt bigger stunts that seriously endanger innocent pedestrians and other road users. Dangerous drivers have even been filmed waving at cameras.

ABC's live broadcast tracked O J Simpson's white 4x4, which is shown here in the middle of the picture.

Case study:
O J Simpson car chase

In 1994, American football star O J Simpson was suspected of murdering his wife. When he failed to turn himself in to the Los Angeles Police Department, the police tracked him down to a white Ford Bronco vehicle being driven by a close friend. However, Simpson threatened to commit suicide, so instead of stopping the vehicle the police followed it for over two hours in a low-speed chase across Los Angeles.

The media soon picked up the story, and by the time Simpson gave himself up over a dozen helicopters had filmed the chase, with some networks interrupting their usual broadcasts to bring audiences live coverage. Thousands of people lined bridges and overpasses to watch the Ford Bronco drive past, and it is estimated that around 95 million viewers watched news footage of the event.

ABCNEWS LIVE COVERAGE
OJ SIMPSON'S CAR

Balanced
reporting

Most news organisations, such as CNN, the BBC and the Australian Broadcasting Corporation, aim to report the facts and offer a balanced view of events. Audiences want to feel that they are getting 'the truth'. But balanced reporting is a difficult thing to achieve. What appears impartial to some may seem heavily biased to others.

Bias in the news

Many news organisations are privately owned. These organisations may be less concerned with impartiality. Their owners may have strong political views and they seek to reach audiences who share their views. They may also try to influence public opinion by employing journalists and commentators who support their version and opinion of events, while giving fewer opportunities to those who oppose them.

Selective reporting

This bias can be seen in the media's reporting of crime statistics. These

Different newspapers reflect different views about crime, its causes and effects.

statistics come from a variety of sources and are often very detailed. So a news outlet will often select a small sample. It may 'cherry-pick' the figures that make the most exciting news story, or it may select only those statistics that support its view and the presumed view of its audience. For example, if a news organisation supports the government it will probably try to show that crime is falling – evidence that the government is doing a good job. If a news organisation opposes the government then it may try to show that crime is rising – evidence that the government's policies are failing.

Bias can also be seen in the types of crime highlighted by a particular newspaper or TV channel.

Case study: Talk radio

'Talk radio' is a phrase used to describe radio shows in which the host discusses topical issues with members of the public who phone in to air their views. One popular US talk show is hosted by Rush Limbaugh, a conservative, right-wing commentator whose success is based partly on his confrontational approach to controversial issues. He frequently accuses other journalists of a liberal, left-wing bias and argues for a firm response to crime. In defence of capital punishment, also known as the death penalty, he has said that 'the only cruel thing about it is the last-minute stays' (reprieves for prisoners).

Rush Limbaugh makes no secret of his views and regularly ridicules liberal attitudes to crime on his show.

• Up for discussion •

Some journalists just investigate and deliver the news, while others give their opinions and speculate about it. What responsibilities, if any, does a journalist or commentator have in the presentation of stories about crime?

Hidden bias

Political bias is not a crime, but other types of bias spread real hatred and are much less acceptable to most people. Homophobia, bias against minority groups such as homeless people or immigrants, and racial prejudice may be concealed or exercised more subtly by the media, the police or the general public.

Race and the police

The police face a difficult task in avoiding claims of racial prejudice. They are required to be 'colour blind' – treating every person in the same way, regardless of race. However, they are sometimes accused of exercising discriminatory policies or allowing racist views. The accidental deaths of two teenagers of North African origin in Paris in 2005 were blamed by some on the fact that they were being chased by police who allegedly singled out young immigrants for harassment. Rioting in several French cities followed, fanned by media coverage.

Media provocation

There are many ways in which the media can provoke or inflame existing prejudices. In a suburb of Sydney,

During the riots in France in 2005, images such as this burning vehicle revealed what was happening, but also helped to spread fear amongst the general population.

Australia in 2005, tensions between local and immigrant youths, sparked off by an alleged attack on two lifeguards, escalated after the circulation of anonymous text messages calling on the white population to attack those of Middle Eastern appearance. The growing violence attracted extensive media coverage which showed images of racist posters and slogans as the rioting gathered pace. After the events, the radio talk show host Alan Jones was found to have breached the race code of the Australian Communications and Media Authority by broadcasting material likely to encourage violence against people of Middle Eastern origin.

Anti-racism protesters marched peacefully through Sydney, Australia after the race riots of 2005.

Case study: Riots in Los Angeles

In 1991, a speeding black motorist named Rodney King was stopped in Los Angeles and severely beaten by four white police officers. A member of the public videoed the beating and this footage caused outrage around the world. The Los Angeles Police Department was accused of institutionalised racism. However, in 1992 the four officers concerned were cleared of assault. Riots immediately broke out across the city. In the aftermath of the riots, some media outlets were accused of editing the video of the beating to leave out evidence that Rodney King was resisting arrest. Others were accused of sending out black journalists to report on the riots at the height of the violence, while relying on white commentators in the studio to pass judgement on events.

• Up for discussion •

Why do you think that the video of Rodney King may have been edited by news organisations? What kind of edits do you think might have taken place? What effects might such editing have?

Glamorising crime

Books, films and TV programmes have a long history of making heroes out of criminals. Highwaymen, the Mafia, gangland – these worlds are made to seem exciting, risk-taking, even romantic. Weapons are glamorised and criminals are shown 'beating the system'.

Criminals become celebrities

Serious crimes generate large amounts of media coverage. We see a criminal's face on the news, we become familiar with their story and the criminal becomes famous. Sometimes this means they can build a career out of their new-found notoriety. A financial trader called Nick Leeson caused the collapse of Barings Bank in Singapore in 1995 after defrauding the bank of millions of pounds in order to cover up previous mistakes. He was sentenced to six and a half years in prison, but what he had done had made him famous. He wrote a book about his experiences, which was made into a film called *Rogue Trader*. Leeson's official website now describes his 'incredible life story' and how he has become 'one of the world's most in-demand conference and after-dinner speakers'.

Nick Leeson is escorted past the waiting media on his arrival back in the UK after his prison sentence.

• *Up for discussion* •

Why do you think some people see criminals as glamorous?

What criminals can you think of that the media has made into sympathetic, even romantic figures?

Rap music in the news

Rap music, garage and hip hop have often been accused of glorifying guns and violence. The work of artists like Snoop Dogg appears to condone petty gangsters, drugs and the necessity of guns with lyrics such as these from his album 'Da Game Is To Be Sold' (Priority Records, 1998):

Nothing left to do, but buy some
shells for my Glock [gun]
Why? so I can rob every known dope
spot [...]
I got 19 dollars and 50 cents up in my
pocket with what?
With this automatic rocket
Gotta have it to pop it, unlock it, and
take me up a hostage...

However, the artists and their promoters deny that there is a link between lyrics about violence and an increase in gun crime.

Case study: 50 Cent

50 Cent is one of many successful US rap artists whose lyrics are supposed to reflect the violent reality of their lives. 50 Cent was dealing drugs aged 12, and in 2000, aged 25, he was shot nine times at close range. He has also been stabbed and involved in several other violent disputes. When a film about his life was criticised for glamorising gun crime, 50 Cent responded by pointing out that many films depicted weapons in their promotional material and that Get Rich Or Die Tryin' *was no different. The controversy ensured extra publicity for the film, but some people think he should not profit from his criminal background.*

Artist 50 Cent's poster for his film *Get Rich Or Die Tryin'* has caused controversy because it shows him with both a gun and a baby.

Fiction or real life?

Crime sells. Sometimes it seems as if we can't get enough of it. As well as all the 'true' crime in the news, we read crime novels, watch films and TV dramas about crime, or play video games in which we can actually 'take part' in graphic scenes of violence. But is all this exposure to fictional crime affecting our attitudes towards real crime?

Cop shows

TV shows about police officers, crimes and procedures have always been popular. However, in recent years, the proliferation of hard-hitting dramas such as *The Wire* or shows such as *CSI* appear to present gritty, harsh reality to audiences who may know very little about policing in the real world. Many characters are either corrupt, or mavericks working outside official procedure. These shows do not always show the painstaking, monotonous, often boring nature of most police investigations and some commentators suggest that they distort our view of the justice system, giving us false expectations or making us unduly cynical about effective policing.

Violent computer games

Video or computer games are not like TV in that the viewer can actually participate in 'virtual' violence. Because of this type of participation and because of the potentially addictive

UK retailer Dixons removed *Manhunt* from its stores in 1994 after the parents of teenager Stefan Pakeerah (see opposite) blamed the violent video game for their son's murder.

Case study: Murder at Columbine

On 20 April 1999, teenagers Eric Harris and Dylan Klebold went on an armed rampage at Columbine High School in Colorado, USA, killing 12 students and a teacher before shooting themselves. Investigations into the massacre revealed video tapes showing one of the killers with a sawn-off shotgun that he called 'Arlene' – allegedly after a character in the computer game, Doom. The families of the Columbine victims tried to sue 25 companies who made similar computer games, arguing that they were partly to blame for turning vulnerable children into 'monster killers'. The case was dismissed, however.

US teenagers Eric Harris and Dylan Klebold were caught on CCTV as they stalked their victims in Columbine High School.

nature of video games, they have been blamed for encouraging aggressive behaviour in some users. In 1994, British 14-year-old Stefan Pakeerah was brutally murdered by a 17-year-old friend after the boys had been playing the adult video game *Manhunt*, in which players score points for violent killings. Stefan's parents and several newspapers blamed the game but no link was ever proved, and the police concluded that the motive was probably robbery.

• *Up for discussion* •

Plenty of people enjoy playing violent video games. Do you think there is any truth in the view that violent video games influence some people to copy such behaviour in real life? Why?

The media
stunt

Campaigners are always seeking publicity for their causes. So some campaigners try to attract attention by staging an event or 'stunt' that the media will find impossible to resist. Sometimes these stunts break the law. But campaigners know that getting arrested is a great way to get their views into the news.

Case study: Plane Stupid

The UK campaign group Plane Stupid has carried out a number of media stunts that have caused widespread disruption and achieved substantial publicity for their cause. Plane Stupid's aims are simple: to further the struggle against airport expansion and greenhouse gas emissions from aviation. In pursuit of their aims, they have occupied a number of airport runways, frequently obstructing aeroplane departures. In 2008 they climbed onto the roof of the British Houses of Parliament, draped banners and chained themselves to the building. On each occasion, the media have documented their actions.

Workmen repair a fence at Stansted Airport in the UK in 2008 after protesters from Plane Stupid broke in and occupied a runway.

• Up for discussion •

Under what circumstances, if any, do you think that campaigners who resort to illegal stunts are ever justified in their actions? Plane Stupid has been given extra publicity in this book by the very fact that their name has been mentioned. Do you think this is acceptable?

Into the picture

Some media stunts are all about getting the right photograph. So the stunt has to be visually exciting or even shocking. Animal rights activists threw a bag of flour over actress Lindsay Lohan outside a nightclub in 2008 because she was wearing fur. Her celebrity status meant that cameras were clicking and the pictures appeared in precisely the sorts of magazines and online sites that the campaigners hoped to target.

Spot the campaigner

Other activists pull high-profile stunts to place themselves in the public eye, for example by scaling public buildings in comic hero outfits (Fathers4Justice), or chaining themselves to equipment used to export coal from Australia (Young People Fight Against Climate Change). Such stunts tend to involve illegal trespass and often end in arrests, but charges are often dropped before the case reaches court.

Actress Lindsay Lohan has attracted the attention of animal rights activists for wearing fur to high profile events, such as film premieres.

Name
and shame

When someone is found guilty of a crime, they are punished. They may be fined, ordered to do community service or sent to prison. But have they learned their lesson? Is there any danger that they might re-offend? The media may decide to publish an offender's name, photograph and sometimes their address alongside details of their crime so that people are made aware of what they have done. They are 'named and shamed'.

A community's right?

Of course, anyone can learn the name of an offender by examining court records or by reading media reports of a case. But 'naming and shaming' is a deliberate attempt to prevent the offender disappearing into the background. For example, some people feel they have the right to know if a sex offender with multiple convictions has moved into their area. They want to be able to protect themselves and their children. However, such information has, at times, led to vigilante attacks against individuals who have already been punished for their crimes.

Drive Drunk...
See Your Mug Shot Here.
Andrew Thomas, County Attorney
©CBS

This billboard in Phoenix, Arizona is designed to deter drink drivers by showing mugshots of convicted offenders.

Case study: A controversial campaign

In 2000, an eight-year-old British girl called Sarah Payne was assaulted and murdered by a convicted sex offender. The UK has no system to alert parents about sex offenders living in their area, unlike 'Megan's Law' which is already in place across the USA. So the News of the World *newspaper began a campaign to 'name and shame' every convicted sex offender in the country by publishing photographs and information about them. The campaign was controversial and was not supported by most child protection groups, who felt that it would merely push convicted offenders into hiding. Also, several innocent men were attacked in cases of mistaken identity. The* News of the World *eventually dropped its campaign.*

• Up for discussion •

Some people argue that the public have a right to know about convicted criminals in their area. Others argue that these offenders have done their time and now have a right to privacy. What's your view?

'Shop a Yob'

It isn't just sex offenders, violent criminals or drink drivers who are targeted by 'naming and shaming'. In the UK, for example, young offenders who are subject to an Anti-social Behaviour Order (ASBO) may find their details in the news. One newspaper ran a 'Shop a Yob' campaign with a hotline for people to provide information about local troublemakers. However, children's rights campaigners have expressed concern about targeting young offenders in this way.

After the murder of UK schoolgirl Sarah Payne, the *News of the World* newspaper asked readers to support its campaign to 'name and shame' convicted sex offenders.

Trial by media

When a serious crime is committed, the media takes advantage of the public's desire for information by offering 24-hour coverage of the story as it unfolds. The crime is examined from every angle. Journalists speculate about what happened, and why. They ask the questions they think the public is asking. This demand can lead to 'trial by media', where the media passes judgement before a trial is concluded in a court.

Collecting evidence needs to be carried out slowly and meticulously.

A quick result

Using the media to keep the public informed has many advantages during a police investigation. The police can appeal for witnesses, alert people to any danger and show that they are following the appropriate procedures. However, detective work can be laborious and time-consuming. The media wants fresh information on a daily or even hourly basis. Journalists may become impatient. They soon start to speculate or question the ability of the police to do their job. In the highly charged atmosphere that follows a crime such as murder, the police are often under pressure to obtain a quick result.

• Up for discussion •

Some people argue that the media is simply doing its job when it speculates about a crime before anyone is convicted.
What do you think?

Case study: O J Simpson murder trial

In 1995, US football star O J Simpson was brought to trial for the murder of his wife and her friend. The case had attracted intense media coverage in the months leading up to the trial (see p.17) and lawyers were concerned that it would be impossible to find an impartial jury — that is, a jury that had not been influenced by speculation in the media.

A jury was eventually chosen and the trial that followed was one of the most publicised in history. TV cameras filmed events inside the courtroom. Polls were broadcast on whether or not members of the public thought O J Simpson was guilty. In the end he was acquitted, but media speculation about the murders and the trial continues to this day.

O J Simpson and his team celebrate after the 'not guilty' verdict is read out.

Flawed evidence

It took three separate trials to convict two brothers of the manslaughter of eleven-year-old Damilola Taylor in London in 2000. This is because the forensic evidence presented by the police at the first two trials was seriously flawed. Critics suggested that forensics teams had been under pressure from the media to find evidence and make arrests. However, significant information leaked to the media also damaged the evidence of key witnesses.

A cause of crime?

Sometimes the media may appear to 'tempt' people into crime. Usually, this is the last thing that editors and journalists intend when they broadcast information or offer a reward. However, by publicising how a crime is committed or how a witness may stand to benefit, they may at times provide the motivation or the means to carry out some crimes.

Copycat crime

Some TV programmes such as *The Real Hustle* specialise in demonstrating how crimes such as fraud or burglary are carried out. Their stated aim is to help members of the public to protect themselves against such crimes. By exposing a conman's technique, for example, audiences can learn how to avoid falling for their scams. But the scams set up by the presenters are generally so entertaining, convincing and successful that some critics have suggested they actually provide a masterclass in how to con innocent people.

The Real Hustle presenters Paul Wilson, Jessica-Jane Clement and Alexis Conran at an awards ceremony.

• *Up for discussion* •

Karen Matthews (see opposite) kidnapped her own daughter because of the prospect of a newspaper reward. Do the media therefore share any responsibility for the crime?

Supporters gather to search for missing schoolgirl Shannon Matthews in her hometown of Dewsbury in 2008.

In February 2008, nine-year-old Shannon Matthews disappeared on her way home from school in Dewsbury in the UK. A huge police investigation began, but some critics accused the media of failing to give her disappearance the same coverage afforded to more well-off families such as the McCanns, whose daughter Madeleine had disappeared in May 2007 while on holiday with her parents in Portugal. Critics maintained that Shannon's story was given less media coverage because she came from a single-parent family from a deprived area of Britain. However, a reward for information was eventually offered by the Sun *newspaper.*

Shannon was found 24 days later, drugged and hidden away at a flat belonging to Michael Donovan, a relative of her mother's boyfriend. However, in the weeks after Shannon's rescue, more details emerged. Shannon's mother, *Karen, had conspired with Michael Donovan to kidnap her daughter, with the intention of 'finding' her in a public place and claiming the reward. Karen was aware of the fund established to help find Madeleine McCann, and hoped to benefit from some of this money herself. Karen Matthews and Michael Donovan were both tried and later imprisoned.*

Graham Dudman, managing editor of the Sun *newspaper, said: 'We will pay big money for the right story and other papers do as well and that's part of a free press... but we don't offer a reward without the complete blessing of the police.'*

Chequebook journalism

Journalists don't just rely on press conferences and court reports for information about a crime. They carry out their own investigations. But journalists don't have to follow strict police procedures. They may decide to pay a witness for an interview or a piece of information. Some people argue that this 'chequebook journalism' is open to abuse.

Exaggerating evidence

One of the problems associated with paying witnesses is that they may be tempted to exaggerate their claims to make their story more exciting and therefore more valuable to the media. Witnesses might also withhold evidence until they see money on the table. They may even make up stories, as with the case of Karen Matthews who 'kidnapped' her own daughter in the hope of getting a reward (see p.33).

The power of money

Some types of 'chequebook journalism' are more open to manipulation than others. For example, a journalist might offer money to a witness to tell their story, but only if the case ends in the conviction of the accused. So the witness might decide to withhold any evidence that casts doubt on a guilty verdict. On the other hand, people may offer bribes to journalists to tell a story in a certain way or not publish it at all.

China's media has been accused of accepting bribes from government officials and business managers who wish to halt any investigation into failure or poor performance.

Case study: The Beckham 'kidnap' case

In 2002, a British newspaper 'uncovered' a plot to kidnap Victoria Beckham, former pop star and wife of footballer David Beckham. But the trial of the alleged plotters collapsed the following year when the court heard how the News of the World *had paid £10,000 to a convicted criminal to tell his version of events. The newspaper argued that it had uncovered the plot after a thorough and legitimate investigation and that no information was withheld from the police. However, the judge in the case decided that the witness's evidence was unreliable as he had been paid for it. It is not illegal for journalists in the UK to pay witnesses for their stories, but the issue remains controversial and many media organisations have now agreed to a voluntary ban.*

 David and Victoria Beckham with their children in 2009. The Beckhams have to be aware of their security at all times and employ a number of bodyguards.

• Up for discussion •

Some people argue that payments to witnesses are sometimes the only way to obtain information on a crime. Perhaps some witnesses deserve financial compensation for their bravery in coming forward. What do you think?

Under surveillance

Cameras are everywhere. CCTV cameras watch us in public spaces. Mobile phone cameras mean that we can take pictures or make videos whenever we like. These images are increasingly used as evidence when a crime is committed, while CCTV is also a tool in crime prevention. But some think that all this surveillance intrudes into our private lives.

CCTV and crime

The success of CCTV in crime prevention and detection depends on cameras working properly. The UK has more security cameras than any other country in Europe, yet in 2008 the British police warned that only three per cent of street robberies in London were solved using CCTV images. They pointed out that there was no fear of CCTV because people assume the cameras aren't working, or that they

• *Up for discussion* •

Does the presence of CCTV make you feel safer? Some people feel that its intrusion into ordinary people's lives is too great a price to pay. What's your view?

CCTV is often seen as a tool in the prevention of crime – thieves may not risk being caught on camera.

aren't positioned correctly. However, CCTV has also been used to track the movements of criminals or witnesses in a number of high-profile crimes such as the Columbine shootings (see p.25). The images don't prevent the crimes taking place, but they can show what happened and who was involved.

Onto the Internet

Images may provide evidence of crimes, but sometimes the presence of cameras can motivate people to commit crime. Cameras on mobile phones have led to a form of bullying called 'happy slapping' where someone is assaulted and the incident is filmed and shared on the Internet. There are issues too about the way CCTV footage is monitored, and who has access to it. For instance, should CCTV images of suspects be placed on the Internet by the police before a court has found them innocent or guilty?

Case study: The shooting of Jean Charles de Menezes

On 7 July 2005, four suicide bombers detonated devices on public transport in London, killing 52 people and injuring over 700. The police recovered 6,000 hours of CCTV footage that provided evidence about the bombers and their movements. Then a second bomb plot was foiled on 21 July 2005. The following day, London police shot and killed Jean Charles de Menezes, believing him to be one of the failed bombers. But they had made a terrible mistake. Jean Charles de Menezes was innocent.

Police surveillance had completely failed to establish Jean Charles de Menezes' identity. However, CCTV footage shown at his inquest helped to establish the truth about what

CCTV images show Jean Charles de Menezes ('JC') as he walked through a London underground station just before he was shot dead in July 2005.

happened. The cameras provided vital evidence that he had not acted suspiciously or jumped over a ticket barrier, as the police had claimed.

Crime online

In recent years, the Internet has become a focus for many types of crime. The nature of this 'new media' means that information can be exchanged, infiltrated, manipulated and downloaded around the world at the press of a button. Crimes such as hacking, identity theft and fraud can cross national borders and become very difficult to trace. The police and other law enforcement agencies are struggling to catch up.

Case study: Cyber attack

In 2007, broadcasters and government departments in Estonia were bombarded by electronic requests for information which overwhelmed their computer servers and caused many systems to crash. The incident was seen as a deliberate attack on the country's infrastructure that appeared to originate from Russia. Media headlines spoke of a 'cyber war', but the involvement of Russian officials has never been proved and only one person has actually been convicted of a crime as a result of the attacks. However the incident has highlighted the vulnerability of electronic data and the need for international cooperation in protecting it from criminals and terrorists.

A few basic precautions such as installing a firewall and other software can help us avoid becoming victims of crime online.

Access all areas?

Most of us want to limit access to 'private' details such as bank statements, emails, browsing history and Facebook profiles for reasons of security or privacy. But all of this data is useful to criminals who want to infiltrate aspects of our lives. Paedophiles and sex pests use false identities to approach children online, while information such as a home address and who lives there can be used by burglars or identity thieves.

The Internet is like a huge public announcement system. Policing it is difficult and users need to take care over the kinds of data they place there.

Phishing

Phishing is a type of deception carried out online. Fraudsters send people unsolicited emails asking for bank details and security codes. Often the emails are made to look and sound like official requests from banks or government departments. When a victim replies, the fraudster uses the data to steal money from their online account. It is important to remember that a real bank would never ask for such details online. However, installing anti-spyware software can help to block phishing emails.

• Up for discussion •

In most countries, the law is changing to allow law enforcement agencies access to private emails, Facebook accounts and text messages. They argue that this is vital for catching criminals. Others argue that this is an invasion of privacy and may be open to abuse. What do you think?

Power
and influence

The media wields immense power to spread information and influence public opinion. This includes our views on crime and our fears about it. However, without an audience the media has no power. So its response to crime is influenced by what we – the public – want.

What do people want?

A 2008 survey by the New South Wales Bureau of Crime Statistics in Australia found that most people vastly overestimated the number of violent crimes committed and underestimated conviction rates for assault and home burglary. Some experts have concluded that the media is to blame for presenting a distorted picture of crime and the ability of the police and courts to deal with it. After all, crimes such as insurance fraud or benefit fraud and stories about low crime rates aren't very exciting. But is the media merely responding to a public interest in stories about violent crime?

Into the future

As the Internet and digital media grow, so traditional newspapers appear to be in decline. Some people fear that this means the end of properly investigative reporting, where journalists are able to

Crime dramas such as *CSI* are hugely popular, but do they provide a realistic assessment of the most common types of crime?

• Up for discussion •

Some people think the media abuses its power, distorting our views about crime. Other people think that the media simply reflects the public interest. What issues in his book have been of most concern to you?

Case study: Making it local

Crime mapping is a recent innovation that combines web-based maps with local crime statistics to provide information about crime in different neighbourhoods. Sites such as www.everyblock.com are increasingly able to provide a crime map not only of individual US cities, but specific streets and blocks. Such innovations are already making an appearance in other countries including the UK, where local government and police are seeking to establish stronger connections between the public and the justice system.

spend weeks or even months digging out facts and interviewing witnesses to establish an independent perspective. Picture-led TV news is still a major force, though our demand for 24-hour coverage can dilute some of its power. But while the Internet can appear to distort crime coverage and focus on the more sensational stories, there are other signs that it can be a useful tool in spreading information about crime, particularly at a local level.

You can have your say on the media by becoming part of it. Set up a blog, write for an online newspaper or post a report on a video-sharing website in response to crime stories in your area.

 David Cameron, the UK Conservative Party leader, demonstrates crime mapping in London.

London ward, April 2008: burglary, robbery & vehicle crime

Glossary

Acquitted Found not guilty of a crime.

Biased Weighted in favour of one side over another.

Capital punishment The death penalty; sentenced to death.

Car jacking Holding up a vehicle and stealing it, often after threatening the driver.

CCTV Closed circuit television.

Con Deceiving or tricking someone for financial gain.

Crime mapping A map showing the type, location and number of crimes in a particular area.

Crime wave A noticeable rise in a particular type of crime.

Deter To try to prevent something, such as a crime, from taking place.

Discriminatory Putting someone at an unfair disadvantage on the basis of race, religion, gender or age.

Documentaries Factual, investigative TV programmes or films.

Editing Piecing together different elements of a written report or film footage; making cuts to a written report or film footage.

Fictional Made up; not true.

Firewall Software used to protect a computer against hackers and unwelcome intrusions.

Forensic evidence Physical evidence, such as blood or cloth fibre, that can be tested by scientists and used in a trial.

Fraud Deception, often for financial gain.

Hacking Using computer technology to gain access to someone else's private information.

Homophobia Fear or dislike of homosexual people.

Identity theft Illegal use of someone else's personal details such as name and address.

Impartial Balanced; fair; without bias.

Institutionalised racism Where the policies and procedures of an organisation such as the police are prejudiced against certain ethnic groups.

Inquest An inquiry into the circumstances of someone's death.

Law-abiding Living within the law; not criminal.

Maverick Someone who breaks the rules or goes against the popular view.

Name and shame Publishing photos, names and other personal details about people who have broken the law.

News blackout A decision not to publish or broadcast a particular news item, often for reasons of safety or security.

Phishing Sending unsolicited emails disguised as official requests for information such as bank details in order to steal money.

Prejudice Fear or dislike of a particular group of people on the basis of race, sexuality, background, religion or nationality.

Press conference Delivering an announcement to a group of journalists; answering journalists' questions.

Producer Programme-maker.

Ratings Audience figures; number of people watching or listening to a broadcast.

Re-enactment A reconstruction of a crime with actors taking the roles of victims, witnesses and criminals.

Speculate Make a guess on the basis of limited evidence.

Statistics Numbers; percentages.

Stereotype A cliché; a limited view of someone.

Stunt An event or action designed to gain maximum attention.

Surveillance Watching, for example via CCTV.

Talk radio A type of radio show where audience members phone in and debate topical issues with presenters and their guests.

Terrorist Someone who seeks to spread fear and panic through violence or who uses violence to gain publicity for a cause.

Vandalism Illegal damage to property.

Vigilante Someone who takes the law into their own hands.

Witness Someone who is present during a crime and can give evidence about what happened to the police and the courts.

Further information

Books

21st Century Debates: Violence in Society by Ronda Armitage (Wayland, 2005)

Issues Today: Crime by Lisa Firth (Independence Educational Publishers, 2008)

What's Your View? Dealing with Crime by Judith Anderson (Franklin Watts, 2005)

Websites

www.homeoffice.gov.uk/crime-victims
This government site provides the latest crime figures, along with advice on what to do if you are a victim of crime.

www.shadowcs.co.uk
This is an interactive site introducing the *Crime Stoppers* concept to young people aged 11–18 through games and discussions.

www.bbc.co.uk/crimewatch
Find out about the BBC's *Crimewatch* programme, how it is made and how reconstructions are put together.

www.met.police.uk/computercrime
The site for the Computer Crime Unit of the Metropolitan Police.

www.newsoftheworld.co.uk/news/campaigns/save_our_streets
This is the website for the *News of the World* newspaper's Save Our Streets campaign – find out about the types of crime that receive most coverage.

www.realhustle.com
A guide to the real-life hustles and scams people fall victim to every day.

http://maps.met.police.uk/
The UK Metropolitan Police site for crime mapping in the Greater London area.

Note to parents and teachers: Every effort has been made by the Publishers to ensure that these websites are suitable for children, that they are of the highest educational value, and that they contain no inappropriate or offensive material. However, because of the nature of the Internet, it is impossible to guarantee that the contents of these sites will not be altered. We strongly advise that Internet access is supervised by a responsible adult.

Index

Numbers in bold refer to captions to illustrations.

These are the list of contents for each title in *Media Power*.